An Atheist's Book of Prayers

An Atheist's Book of Prayers

Poems by

Wesley R. Bishop

© 2025 Wesley R. Bishop. All rights reserved.
This material may not be reproduced in any form, published,
reprinted, recorded, performed, broadcast,
rewritten or redistributed without
the explicit permission of Wesley R. Bishop.
All such actions are strictly prohibited by law.

Cover design by Shay Culligan
Cover image by Wesley R. Bishop
Author photo by Wesley R. Bishop

ISBN: 978-1-63980-827-4

Kelsay Books
502 South 1040 East, A-119
American Fork, Utah 84003
Kelsaybooks.com

To Allison, always.

Acknowledgments

I owe special thanks to my friends and colleagues Ricardo Quintana-Vallejo, Carmine Di Biase, Lindsay Holman, Marc Valle, and Leslie Worthington for reading through these pieces and offering notes at different stages.

Also, Jessica Cory and Willie Carver read through the entire finished manuscript to provide blurbs. Both are talented editors and writers in their own right, and I thank them for taking the time to do this.

I also want to thank the editors and staff of the following journals where some of the poems first appeared.

Appalachian Journal: "Homeric Greek," "Vandal Beheads Controversial Statue of Mary Giving Birth Inside Austrian Cathedral, July 3, 2024."
Pine Mountain Sand & Gravel: "Field Life."
Querencia: "Labor," "Fated," "Saved."

Finally, I thank Allison, my friend, partner, and first reader.

Contents

Field Life	13
Homeric Greek	14
Saved	15
Abraham	16
Insured	17
Alabama Walmart	18
Hercules	20
An Atheist's Prayer	21
Freckles	22
Nothing Else	23
Vandal Beheads Controversial Statue of Mary Giving Birth Inside Austrian Cathedral, July 3, 2024	24
Talking to Spiders in Dreams	25
Porch	27
Soup	28
Labor	29
Remainder Drives	30
Dead Angry Thing	31
Fat Stomach	32
Fat Man	33
Belly	34
Sky in Appalachia	35
Atlanta	36
Sandwich	37
Flies	38
Ant	39
Online	40
American Laments	41
Violent	42
Waterborne	43
Gaza	44

Light Eaters	45
Fated	46
Manifest	48
Cyborg	50
America, Yes	51
Praying with No Belief	52
Jesus	53
Red Clay	54
Spanish	55
Meta's AI Explains a Sex Joke	57
Ant II	58
My Father In-Law is Angry at the Robot Taking His Call	59
Relative Humanity	60
Quintard Avenue	61
Joe Biden's Inaugural Address: Erasure Poem	62
Midwest	64
Envelope	65
Physical Therapy	66
Blue Birds	67
Alabama Plot	68
River Dam	69
Computing	70
Leaf	71
Thomas Jefferson	72
A Good Mother	73
Morning Glories	74
A Civil War	75
Shattered	77
Lake	78
Obamacare	79
Duckling	80

Learned	81
Learned More	82
Learn This Please	84
Arson	85
Where We Break	86

Field Life

I imagined a god that was not hateful
and in so doing, unimagined America.

What plains would swell to life
minus that persistent divine?

What sounds, so grateful,
like a dragonfly's wings liberated,

would beat amidst cold grass' knife,
edging closer to closeted grove's dark?

No more cotton fields, harsh white, in full.
Just a tame wild clearing where America

was
had been,

an Atlantis fallen to grasslands bountiful.

Homeric Greek

We forget
that Homeric Greek
was used to tell
a people about their past.

Rarified knowledge
in class halls
echoing with lectures

came later.

So, I talk
in Appalachian English,
Midwest seasoned.

Because I do not know
how else to tell
our stories.

Saved

Jesus revival in Walmart parking lot,
"Jesus Saves!" gospel singers inform.
But, too,
"Save at Walmart!" signs declare.

Those cart wranglers
push silver mounts,
causing me to duck

when I hear
BANG!

gun . . . gun . . . gun . . .

I fret,
but fear not,
just carts, temporarily

out of control.

What do I have to worry?
We are all going to be saved . . .

saved . . . saved . . . .. saved . . .

because somewhere, somewhen
a coupon
was nailed to a cross.

Abraham

What if god had commanded Abraham
to have an abortion? Would you say
submit to divine will then?
And if "no," then suppose you find your will
superior more
than that of a god. And if so, then suppose,
that human will more divine. So, who are we to say
what is wrong or right
in people planning parenthood?

Insured

By the road,
where the injury lawyers' signs rise,
the kudzu spreads.
Green wild limits on the outskirts of town with no bold
celebrations

just things growing, things dying,

just the green goodness suffocating structures, flailing
in living waves.

Alabama Walmart

There are poems everywhere. In Walmart in Alabama when you stop and smell the baking aisle and all manner of things seem possible. Like how you used to stand at your grandmother's buffet and read the Bible passages from the large illustrated edition she owned.

"Who's that?" you'd ask pointing to the picture of a man enraged and pushing pillars down to the alarm of all around. You were afraid of that man. You were afraid of that rage. You had heard of it before, rumors really, it was whispered about in familial proverbs about how Grandpa sometimes was not himself.

To be careful.

Your Grandmother wiped her hands, switched places with you, and handed you the fork so you could do the crisscross, pushing the balls of sweet, salty goodness down. She looked at the picture and told you the story of Sampson and Delilah.

Betrayal. Rage. Hair with magical, mystical properties. You listened to that story in rapture, realizing that the story wasn't "real," but a poem meant to tell you something more Truth than mere reality.

In Walmart in Alabama you think of that day as a woman walks up to you in the baking aisle. She is asking for help finding vegetable juice but begins sobbing, apologizing, and sobbing again. You ask if you can help as you see bruises form, so fresh they have not been concealed. She says that her husband just beat her and that she does not want the cops called and that she just needs "fucking vegetable juice!"

Why are things so hard, she asks?

You point her to the correct aisle and think about Sampson's rage and grandfathers now dead, now conveniently remembered happily. "He was a good man!" People say on Facebook every year at the anniversary of his death.

You worry, oh do you worry, about that woman leaving your side, and you wish that you could do more like Sampson, avenging others who have had their hair and dignity cut.

But you can't. You couldn't as a kid at a buffet reading the Bible, and you can't now, with all of your fancy degrees. All you can do, it seems, is put it down in a poem.

Because those are everywhere.

Hercules

What if Hercules were aborted?
Jesus never carried to term?
Would gods, with their entitled cocks,
have learned the meaning of consent sooner?
Where bodies of others
were not canvases for divine manifestation?

I doubt (event then)
the idea would have taken root.
Marbled halls in misty clouds
up above lived soil do not lend
to lessons well.

So, do not pray
for respect and dignity.
Take it.
It's yours, not by divine will,
but simple choice.

An Atheist's Prayer

I want to pray to the god of beautiful things, of wisteria in trees and abandoned buildings, faded lavender and fainter scents, but I am an atheist, and do not pray.

My fellow Americans pray to a myriad of things, many not being atheists, I marvel at their gods. There are so many. There are gods even of the cruel things, best left unsaid but somehow always spoken.

Their followers build altars and say the names of gods of cruel things in time rushing.

Online. Offline. On TV, from pulpits to state legislatures.
And I keep looking at wisteria. And public places. And I wonder if these gods I am seeing care what their siblings are doing?

Clasp my hands, not in prayer, but for sanitizer.

Amen.

Freckles

There is a love letter in the surprise
of a stranger's face looking up from a book
or turning in line and greeting with splashes
of unexpected freckles, crowning cheeks, cresting

smile.

The world may perish,
but then again no,
those freckles, like gold dandelions, claim
highway spaces,
        grow—not in spite—despite
imperial planned green tracts, persisting points, praying

abound.

Nothing Else

The barista pumps his press,
his strong arms working,
while the cashier's red hair glows,
and the light, I think, must be for that glowing,
and nothing else, she is so beautiful.

There is green clover
amidst Alabama brown spring grass,
yards not fully recouped for growth,
and I think, the light must be for that growing,
and nothing else, all so bountiful.

But I cannot connect to it all,
except when I do, limbs shocking,
I am a lineman thrown to wires pulsing,
my mind losing control and spiraling,
and nothing else, I am so lost.

How to replant after a slash and burn?
I don't think I can, I have nothing left,
and nothing else, despite it being oh, so
beautiful.

Vandal Beheads Controversial Statue of Mary Giving Birth Inside Austrian Cathedral, July 3, 2024

It is grotesque to see how a woman
birthed a god with her body.

Violate that woman's work.
And let us crown the Jesus-God
without witnessing
the actual crowning.

Talking to Spiders in Dreams

Do you talk
to the spiders you see
in your dreams?

I do,
although
I know
it is not
popular
to admit.

But you'll find
in those conversations divine
that spiders are

surprisingly
good
conversationalists.

Their logic is different than ours
(of course).
They're predators

and
        solitary
and
        when I meet them we

always seem to chat
about the virtues
and
        vices

of

        Prey, Praying, Prayer

past tense, gerunds, and other matters of grammatical form.

"Our language, you see,"
I tell the Queen of the Spiders,
"is like a web.

You have to be careful
you do not step on the wrong word,
Stick!"

She, the grand beautiful spider, nods
in understanding
and
        we spin more meaning

            spin, spin, spin

until daylight reclaims my thoughts,
knocks loose those cobbled webs
of silken stanzas.

Porch

There is a patch of porch that holds the heat of the previous day, hours after the earth has turned again.

When I step out in evening to open doors and allow smoke to escape from my dinner attempts,

I feel that heat meet my soles.

I wonder what other sensations my shoes hide, before reminding myself that they protect me to enjoy this very moment, soaking the surprise vestiges of a yesterday.

Soup

Love is pouring broth
together
as she and I near the bottom of separate bowls
so, our soup lasts longer,
sipping flavors
newly mixed.

Labor

Alabama on my mind
as passing by
prison-labor on roadside
beautifying dividers green.

Pants are orange and white,
stripped to show
reflecting light.

Alabama, ever the genius
in stealing labor not their own.

Remainder Drives

The leaves are rusting and sway
like barn doors hinging,
badly maintained but swearing
to swing back into place
after breeze's fit settles.

Those leaves promise
yet cannot fulfill forever
the place they hold

and this is why when friends tell me
they go for autumn drives after funerals unexpected
I say it is best to play music too.

The melodies fade but can keep promises
and are on command with a simple touch.

Dead Angry Thing

I left my anger to lie fallow like a dead wild animal found in a field, the type of corpse that is a morning surprise as you make the rounds from barn to sheds. Its broken body will be a conversation, at least, until noon day meal.

Conventional wisdom said I should remove it, immediately, lest the wildness seep into that cultivated soil, the untamed tang fermenting the seed.

But I did not have the heart to do so. Less radioactive than fatally wounded, I dared not disturb the wronged in death, and instead tied soda cans to baler-twine-string to hear if, and when, something would come and ingest the remains, heal the earth that is, in my stead.

Fat Stomach

When your father in-law grabs your stomach with fist, digging nails into flesh, and says loudly so all can hear, "You need to do something about this," you remember the time, years ago when you were forced to live out of your car, sleeping in parking lots, showering at truck stops. It was a time of danger; you knew even then. Not a crossroad but the center of a compass rose bloom wilting in summer heat. A professor had asked after lecture hall cleared, "Why are you falling asleep in class?" You did not have the words for how to say hands felt wrapped around neck, air and light disappearing. The professor proceeded to care, no to damn, and you remember why you made school a home so many times in your life. Real family in library stacks and meetings and research papers. Anyway, that is what you think of as you wonder if it would be okay to punch the familial fucker in the mouth who holds your stomach, holds your body hostage.

Fat Man

In films
when a character says,
"That could be a 300-pound dude! You don't know!"
to prove a point about the dangers of online dating,
I can't help but think,

what makes you think my fine fat ass
would ever want to date you online or in-person?

Belly

I love how my belly feels
as it rests on my thighs
sitting here in morning calm
before campus blooms to life

in contrast to autumn trees
emptying foliage to be bare.

I no longer drink coffee,
bad for those merciful nerves,
so, it is tea that soothes my throat
and my belly that bumps
table in rising for the day.

Sky in Appalachia

The clouds, low this morning,
crash into mountains.
The rain sounds as exploding buttons
from a ripping shirt
held together no more.

Atlanta

Folks say Atlanta
is a modern Mecca.
But then I think,
isn't Mecca the modern Mecca?

Like how Rice
is the supposed
Harvard of the South,
and wheat, I suppose,
the rice of Kansas.

But does Harvard ever say
it is the Rice of Massachusetts?

I bow my head in prayer,
the ancient texting,
facing Talladega and beyond—

"Dear god, u up? Wat u doin?"

Sandwich

Cutting it in half
is how you say, "I love you,"
in sandwich.

Flies

The flies that gather around sugar bowl hold conference
like the friends at a funeral who agree on your character
and enclave their words so as to limit conflicts
you held in life and in so doing conflict
between biography and last rite hymns.

Ant

The morning ant
on tea saucer clean antennae
for day's work.

Online

I walk digital corridors
and in one frame people scream
in pain from genocide.

In another frame, recipes,
for holiday cookies, and those are accompanied
by recycled music.

In a third, a paid boosted post screams
it is CHRISTMAS, not HOLIDAY,
with recycled rage.

And I think, this is not new.
This has always been the world.
Connected but not.

And I walk on, Mr. Globe that I am,
until one day when I'm not.

American Laments

America could be beautiful if it were not here, not this when, and it is why, I at least pretend, that so many poets write in abstract meaning with concrete examples.

You wail along and lament how beautiful our era could have, should have, would have been if we were somewhen else.

Violent

Outlaw the violent.
Legalize the erotic.

This needs to be
an age of love.

We have had our fill
full of violence with no abandon.

It is time we love
and abandon no more

the promise we made
to each other

to be violets, wild
growing into purple

repose.

Waterborne

My department chair tells me coastal elites are to blame

(for everything)

but every time I approach the ocean
all I meet
are Uber drivers and waitresses
working multiple jobs
while my dean back home rakes in six figures,
tells me research trips can't be funded,

(go figure)

and the landlord demands his payment,
again, it's a new month.

Maybe inequality
is not waterborne.

Gaza

America,
where is Biden?
He is in the missiles,
bellowing "GM lives,
and bin Laden is dead!"

America rains down,
thank the gods
bipartisanship thrives,

in the regrowth amidst rubble,
choking vines that grow strong

on the bodies of those we do not see.

Light Eaters

I want to be a plant
feasting on sunlight
and exhaling cool air.

Naysayers nay and say
no, not possible
because like solar panels

I'd die at night, no power.

But I don't have power now.
So, why not be vegan ultra
and feast on light?

I'll put a word in with Darwin
and see if he can do
us a solid in the next Ice Age.

Fated

I dreamt last night
that we were all doomed
to die at the stroke of three

(not midnight, far too cliché)

but could be saved if, and only if,
someone uttered your name
and saw you
as worthy
of being
saved.

In those panicked hours
we came to realize how little
celebrity mattered as *Go-Fund-Me* campaigns
for the lonely sprouted like weeds
and name-insurance-plans
assembled.

And we waited to see
who would say whose name

life pacts were formed
and I had her name on my tongue
and she had my name bouncing out
and we hugged and waited,

praying
for the nameless.

Manifest

I've been told
so often I do not know
who to cite
that as an American
I am to dream
of wide-open spaces.

To manifest those dreams
with imperial schemes in a destiny self-evident.
But
I simply don't.

Never have I ever, and as I age in this age
of rapid degradation,
of resegregated hopes,
where some men, #notall,
dream of what to do with billions+
and where some men, #notall,
must dream for simple survival measured
in years, months—temporal inches.

We hold the truths to be self-evident,
that all men, #notallmen,
have same day delivery,
and rush to frontiers,
former, grand, and final.

But I still just want
that quiet place of dignity simple,

residing somewhere beyond
the border's bend.

Cyborg

Cyborg dreams are of merging with tech and is only grotesque, only a nightmare, to the able-bodied, the temporarily non-disabled. For the rest, it is not fantasy far off

it is now,
it is fine.

So much dystopia is willful misunderstanding.

America, Yes

There are two Americas.
        One I'm told about endlessly, the other just where I live.
But that first, endless America feels like it is coming to an end.
    In fact, it is ending before beginning although its narrative has
                                                     been nonstop.
    That first America is an America of movies and textbooks and vowels and consonants bleeding through a continent like a staining liquid seeping through and through
                        cheap napkins.

I've learned to be wary of that first America.
    I do not know how to patty cake a dream, or shimmy lift my hips
                                        to another's story.
I live in just second America, after all.
    The one that is just a place in time. Regions with various zip codes
                                          zipping to and fro.
I am done with dreams of fathers and forefathers, and I need to unsettle my thinking that yes, America is worth fighting for, but not that America first.
                                                    Fuck that place.
An America where we can just be our natural freeway, and do not need reliance on bedtime stories to convince us burning nations are here to stay.

Praying with No Belief

I looked for a gospel I could follow but the pews were all dry with overflowing bodies of words

       confessing water, prescribing fire, and muttering in tongues holy.

And I took myself, body only, leaving soul, and rolled in mortality I had left.

       Shuddered in the knowing that I would end.

Death is not painless, not always. It is often violent and twisted, like pieces of car left after a wreck—

       quick! We sweep up twisted devices no longer working—

and we go back to driving, except those who don't.

And I am one of them who has kept driving, kept going, as so many highway ghosts stare at me

       and ask why I should live?

And there is no answer, because I do not deserve to. I have learned that is the horror and the holy,

       none of us do.

None of this is credit scores earned, but states bequeathed on the unwilling, the begging, those avoiding

       the lack of dignity death brings.

Jesus

What if Jesus is the villain?
  In all our challenges
    HE remains, held but untouched,
      a creepy man we all were told
        we must love
OR ELSE!

  After all he suffered so much

FOR US!

  To not embrace his outstretched arms,
    to question that sacrifice—
      no one asked for, and no one wants—

is to invite his wrath, I'm warned.

What if HE is the villain?
  In splendid, abusive glory
    we cannot see it.
      Wow. What a guy.

Red Clay

The grass's brown
persists, despite rain repeated
and climate mild.

I wonder if things native-not
could take root,
no, not like kudzu,
but softer things that speak
and never shout,

that grow as living bone
after car collision,
and mend like memory,
as red clay does,
beneath the brown grass still.

Spanish

In high school
neither my mother nor my father
would help with Spanish homework.

Handing them the paper of vocabulary
they listened, once each, as I tried to recall
meanings new
and part way through
they handed back the list
and said they could not assist
it was something too foreign,

and years before,
I later learned,
county parents protested when the State
mandated new languages be taught.

Our Spanish teacher, whose son was born
my sophomore year, told us how her husband
forbade the child learn Spanish too.

Now, as a teacher myself, I get coffee with a colleague in mathematics,
we discuss cuts and how language
is no longer required.
Too much complaining from students, parents, government.

I tell her I think the reason so many of our students are

afraid/resistant/hateful

to learn Spanish is racism.
She flutters her white hands,
says that cannot be.
She does not see racism
there.

Meta's AI Explains a Sex Joke

"Do you want five guys?"

The woman is confused by the question, says that is too much.

Then she realizes it's a restaurant, not an orgy being proposed.

"The comments are laughing," the AI states, "with many assuming she was ready to take five men. However, as one commenter points out, she was likely joking, and messing with the other person, and that her quick wit is quite impressive."

None of this funny. The planet burns through the punchline.

Ba-dooo-ssshhh.

Ant II

Ant sips drops
from dripping bottle
in August heat.

My Father In-Law is Angry at the Robot Taking His Call

He cannot tell its race, and so this dulls his swearing, his words use to the ready form of slurs.

Meanwhile, the AM radio prattles in the background wondering, "If we call Republicans 'weird' is that hate speech?"

Relative Humanity

Who have you been trained to see as human and who have you been beaten into seeing as not?

I ask because in order for compassion to work, I need to know what language you speak.

Will the dead fetuses of a Palestinian evoke anger?

Maybe if I wrap their broken bodies in an American flag.

What if I give the dead a professorship in your department?

Will that move you to flutter your lips, give the atrocity a name, provide the relevance for your grief to finally register?

Quintard Avenue

When tomatoes are chilled
they taste like invigorating battery acid
as they mix their juices
with flimsy bread,
slapped together by speeding hands
in the links of chain fast food stores
lining Quintard Avenue.

A young woman leaves
the plasma donation center
where they do not donate,
but sell, blood.
It is one of the more lucrative
lines of work in Anniston.

There is a park between these two scenes,
one that "honors the military legacy,"
of Alabama general or the nation specific,
I'm not sure, due
to the fact that I have never gone.

Joe Biden's Inaugural Address:
   Erasure Poem

We have never, ever, ever failed in America when we have acted together. And so today, at this time and in this place, let us start afresh. All of us. Let us listen to one another. Hear one another. See one another. Show respect to one another. Politics need not be a raging fire destroying everything in its path. Every disagreement doesn't have to be a cause for total war. And, we must reject a culture in which facts themselves are manipulated and even manufactured. My fellow Americans, we have to be different than this. America has to be better than this. And, I believe America is better than this. Just look around.

We have failed listen . Hear . See Politics a raging fire destroying everything in its path total war. we a culture in which facts themselves are manufactured. My fellow Americans, I believe America is this. Just look around.

Midwest

The Midwest,
like a potato chip,
disappoints only
in unrealistic
expectations.

Envelope

I, too, am an envelope,

and like the twilight caught
in tree lines
when sky colors
stratify in zones of night-cold
and day-heat
and the world seems to be an impossible occurrence,
just before bursting past
its paper-glue corners,

I too, spill like the secret
I whispered in your ear
as marbles on pavement.

Physical Therapy

Love is calendar invites from her,
not needing to check
before clicking "ACCEPT"
because there is nowhere
more important to be
than driving her
to early physical therapy
when fog hangs on Cheaha Mountain,
adorning the morning,
as a delicate veil.

Blue Birds

Ohio frost on car, facing north.

I've never seen so many blue birds in one flock.

The trail signs say they are working to restore what was once lost.

And the election signs in yards along the road speak to division.

Alabama Plot

Alabama is not real.
It is a plot device
made by William Faulkner,
or some other Southern gothic mind.

Can you imagine,
how horrible still,
if Alabama were fact
and not a faux box for refuse,
a square of space
to hold all we are
ashamed to see?

River Dam

One summer my cousins and I dammed a small stream that cut across several farms. We chose a place that bent and hollowed deep, and it was both close enough and far enough for us to walk from our grandparents' home.

And that bend filled fast with cool brown, green water. And we swam.

When the adults discovered our act they applauded us, said it was sturdy and ingenious, but that we must tear it down.

As we did the wall of water flooded back along its dried spine.

We did not, they explained, have a right to damn a river.

Computing

What if I'm just a computer, sent to earth by some people from another planet, and my job is to learn about this place so that when I die I'm uploaded back to my home and I can tell the people of another place, what we did here with years granted, like grapes growing ripe on a bowing vine, climbing a tree, hoping to tear nothing down.

Leaf

Leaf hangs by stray web,
already brown for autumn,
aside the calm lake.

Thomas Jefferson

I have had students
angrier with Thomas
for the Jefferson Bible
than his raping of Sally Hemmings
I think
this is the visual aid
I needed to see
for why I hate America so much.

A Good Mother

The gas station attendant yells at the abandoned dog,
eyes hopeful and stomach sagging from too much milk.
I wonder where her pups are?
But the workers of the *Circle K* shout,
"Get on out of here!" And she complies,
trotting as fast as her legs will carry,
as I refuel to drive in the opposite direction.

Morning Glories

Morning glory,
lovely growing
on chain link fence.

Its faded blue
petals,
its explosive yellow
center.

My mother would say it's "invasive,"
chastise those who grew it,
those who tolerated it.

But the morning glory's
persistence,
its aggressive assertion to life,
made me love it all the more
as it charted an existence
along the fake line we drew
about those plots of property.

A Civil War

I am not
an Ulysses,
nor a Sumner.
I am from places
where names,
once dead,
quickly erase.

Those memorials
with dead
listed as
antiquarian
phone books

to Hades

mean nothing,
like Latin
on the lips.

Death rites,
not markers
to living things
that once had arms,
that once had legs,
that once had heads.

So, war,
that center crumbling,
fills me with cold

water, multicolor
from runoff antifreeze.

I know
we have
those parts
to play
instead of reclining
for our
one sacred breath
we are afforded
in union.

Shattered

Dropping that punch bowl,
eyes following its path to shatter
in chaos rivulets of sharp teeth,
awaiting feet
and pursuing no plan to gather
those shards
is all not ideal but real in a way
I've struggled to accept as I walk barefoot
and bereft across the kitchen floor.

Lake

When the lake shallows
in eager autumn
and the geese graze
below the park's too early Christmas lights
I'm reminded of wind
and all it does
speaking trees into our ears
before we forget for several months
that leaves, too, sing.

Obamacare

When my grandfather's heart gave out, the night after Obama Care was passed, after a night of watching Fox News and fuming, I wondered if he knew he had spent the last year of his life already, the last year to meet new people, the last year to attend reunions, the last time the day before, drinking coffee at his favorite McDonalds, down the road from his farm?

Or the last chance to apologize to my dad, that winter before, for the abuse and drunken terror he had visited on him and grandma and uncles and aunts, they huddled decades before, afraid in rooms as he would come back from the bar.

I remember that time, the last chance to make amends, and wonder if he did too, lying in bed clutching his chest?

That past winter he had read a new biography of Chuck Norris. He was telling dad and my girlfriend (he would not live to see us married the next year) about Norris learning martial arts to protect himself from his abusive father, how Norris was, unlike so many celebrities "these days" a good Christian man.

Dad sat at that table and waited, for what I don't know, but something. However, grandfather's book report ended with no self-awareness and my father fumed on and off for days.

And then, death, and then fuming more from the men like grandfather. His casket laid in the grave on hill. And amends still left unsaid, buried in an unremarkable spot in the Ohio River Valley.

Duckling

Duckling
chases rolling pebble
unsure of food
and mouths it,
when caught,
in young beak,
but cannot break
so, drops
and returns to the waddling flock
of fluff and feathers
before wings can strengthen
for migration soon.

Learned

I learned authoritarianism in that house.

How she would, when overwhelmed, with the expectations of an unwanted life, threaten to leave and we'd never see her again, this, she yelled, would be the end of the family, she'd repeat again and again until we screamed and cried enough she, satiated, would put her suitcase back, unpack the wadded clothes thrown, and make us swear to never transgress again.

She did this until one day, I said *fine, leave,* and that I could keep house while dad worked. We would be better off, I said. All of us.

And she hit me with the broom then. Not like a bat, but a battering ram to my thin narrow chest, and it knocked me to the ground. But each time I got up, I could see the fear in her face. The threat evaporated, and how she only had force. And I was one step closer to liberation.

This was my classroom to politics.

The pain of broom thistles on young skin stings, but it felt good and honest and right to hurt. Like sweet raspberries gained from a summer bush, thorns tearing fingertips.

I just wish she'd had the courage
    to leave
        her prison of motherhood.

Learned More

He guilted her into staying.

I remember the fight in the living room,
us huddled in rooms, hoping the words would not turn to fists
aimed at us.

She wanted to leave.

He could not imagine it.

And so, when we were called to the room, he said she was ripping
us all apart.
And my sisters ran to her to cry, scared more for the volume of
voices.

The monsters lurking in words thrown like closet recess.

I watched from the door, already old enough to know
what was happening
to map it like a geographer
she made a calculation then

I saw, I saw, I saw

if she left, she would face an onslaught from him
and given her demeanor
        and his words
we would grow to hate her.

So, she stayed. The family persisted.
And I grew to hate both anyway.

Learn This Please

America is not worth dying for.
America is not worth killing for.
Is America worth living for?
      Also, no.
Yet, see that patch,
over a way,
maybe it has
      promise.

Arson

Your Trump-supporting uncle is no earthquake or flood or swarm
 of locust.
Those are natural things, the stuff adjacent to our human-made
 world.
They do not wish us ill. They simply are.
No, your uncle and grandma and nice neighbor
douse the future in kerosine and light it.
I love the locust and am obligated to learn their calls,
to accept the earth and her weather rupturing.

I do not tolerate the bonfire dances of arsonists.

Where We Break

There is the crying
not of sadness
but of pain,
when your body needs
a carpeted floor to be clay
and break and return
soft
to malleable bonds.

About the Author

Wesley R. Bishop is an assistant professor of American and Public History at Jacksonville State University, Alabama. His previous books include *Liberating Fat Bodies: Social Media Censorship and Body Size Activism* (Palgrave, 2024), *COVID19 Haiku: Short Poems in a Long Year* (North Meridian Press, 2024), and *The Long March of Coxey's Army: The Path of Protest from Populism to the New Deal* (University of Illinois Press, forthcoming). He is the founding and managing editor of North Meridian Press.

www.ingramcontent.com/pod-product-compliance
Lightning Source LLC
Chambersburg PA
CBHW031201160426
43193CB00008B/465